THE COOLIDGE LEGACY

THE *Coolidge* LEGACY

BY

CYRILLA BARR

Library of Congress   Washington   1997

This publication was made possible by a generous donation from Mrs. Reid Denis.

Library of Congress Cataloging-in-Publication Data
Barr, Cyrilla.
      The Coolidge Legacy / Cyrilla Barr.
           p.   cm.
     ISBN 0-8444-0917-0
--- ------ Z663 .C66 1997
      1. Coolidge, Elizabeth Sprague, 1864–1953. 2. Music patrons—United States—
Biography. 3. Library of Congress Elizabeth Sprague Coolidge Foundation. I. Title.
ML29g.B37 no. 1 <Case>   97-19865
780'.92   CIP
[B]—DC21   MN

Cover: Elizabeth Sprague Coolidge, circa 1916.

Endpapers:
A montage of Coolidge materials including:
Coolidge's composition exercise book from the period when she was studying with Arthur Whiting; on one side of the last page there is his comment about the good progress she has made. A letter from Gabrielle D'Annunzio. Coolidge's "Round Robin" containing four bars of music, each with the signature of the composer—Franco Alfano, Alfredo Casella, Mario Castelnuovo-Tedesco, Gian Francesco Malipiero, and Ottorino Respighi—written on the occasion of her departure from Naples after her successful European tour of 1931.
Compositions by Ottorino Respighi, Béla Bartók, Paul Hindemith, Arnold Schoenberg, and Frank Bridge which were commissioned by Elizabeth Sprague Coolidge.

Frontispiece: This photograph of Nan Sprague with her daughter Elizabeth at the age of eight, shows off the fine profile that can be seen to such advantage in many of Coolidge's later pictures.

Contents

A Message from The Librarian of Congress

Whether we are reflecting on the Library's past or looking into its possible futures, we invoke the spirit of the founder of our collections, Thomas Jefferson, who, in his far-reaching curiosity, built a personal library that became the Nation's Library. It is a model that in its scope and depth still inspires us as our power to store and disseminate the numbers, words, and images that comprise the world's tangible memory outstrips our ingenuity in using that power.

Music was not the least among Jefferson's many interests. An accomplished amateur who played the flute for his own enjoyment, and who appreciated the value of music making in the development of a well-rounded individual as well as for the enhancement of social life, his knowledge of the proper selection of instruments for a military band of his time was sufficiently expert for his recommendations to have contributed significantly in the early organization of the U.S. Marine Band. Not surprisingly, then, the Library's holdings of music begin with the 1814 acquisition of Jefferson's library, although the formal establishment of a Music Division had to wait for the completion of the Thomas Jefferson Building just a century ago.

Since then, the Music Division has been the beneficiary of generous patronage, beginning with Elizabeth Sprague Coolidge and continuing on with Gertrude Clarke Whittall (whose contributions included five Stradivarius instruments and funds for the maintenance of a resident string quartet), Dayton C. Miller, Serge Koussevitzky, Leonora Jackson McKim, Ira and Leonore S. Gershwin, and many others. But it is Coolidge, our first great patron, whom we celebrate here. As Jefferson shaped the Library of Congress, Coolidge's gifts, which were as enlightened in their wisdom as they were rich in the material endowments of bricks, mortar, and money, shaped the Music Division—and much of musical life both in America and abroad—as no benefactor has since.

Here is a glimpse of her story, the story of how the vision of one person can become the vision of a great institution.

James H. Billington
The Librarian of Congress

Foreword

This year, 1997, is the centennial of the Music Division of the Library of Congress. The best imaginable present we could share on this occasion is the reopening of the Elizabeth Sprague Coolidge Auditorium, inaugurated on its founder's birthday on October 30, 1925 and dark, or more properly speaking, silent, for nine years during the restoration of the Thomas Jefferson Building, also a hundred years old this year. The Auditorium has now been returned to us, its famous acoustics intact but with its production facilities much improved, for the resumption of free public concerts.

With the building of this historic Auditorium in 1925 and the concurrent donation of funds to support its activities, the U.S. government took the unprecedented step of accepting the administration in perpetuity of a privately endowed foundation. Equally significant is the fact that, upon the establishment of the Coolidge Foundation, the mission of an academic library was joined with that of a commissioning and performing institution so that each of their activities would stimulate and inform the other. Here, notes on paper come to life and we are continually reminded of the relationship between the documents that we conserve as records of the past and the musical rites that we perform as celebration of the present or, *in* the present, of a recreated past. That these two worlds—academia and the conservatory, or scholarship and show business—have anything to do with one another is still by no means universally accepted today, and no other institution has followed the Library's example in this sometimes risky yet continually stimulating and productive experiment, however successful the Library's experience has proven to be over the years.

That Coolidge was aware of the need to take chances is evident from her statement that one of the main purposes of her Foundation was the support of projects that, were their realization to be guided by more practical considerations, might not be attempted. While she insisted on well-established performers of the highest accomplishment, she took chances on commissions even when she expected that she might not like or understand the results. Some of this century's most original and influential music and dance by such artists as Stravinsky, Bartók, Schoenberg, Webern, Hindemith, Prokofiev, Ravel, Sessions, Graham, and Copland, among many others, have been commissioned by the Library's Coolidge Foundation.

Coolidge's support of chamber music was in itself a somewhat risky undertaking, for such a thing was then scarcely known or appreciated in America. She supported it with money, but also with solid musical knowledge, intelligence, vision, and, perhaps most important of all, the capacity to form close friendships, so that her role as a patron of the arts was often deeply personal. Just how active a part she played in the lives of the composers she commissioned, the musicians she employed, and all others with whom she had a working relationship can be only suggested by her letters, diaries, and other documents. Nevertheless, her biographer, Cyrilla Barr, has drawn from them a vivid portrait of a woman to whom all of us whose lives have been enriched by chamber music are indebted beyond calculation, and a woman in whom all may find a model of generosity and courage, which she exemplified both in her personal and her public lives.

This is Dr. Barr's brief account—a much longer one is to be published next year—of Coolidge's long and fruitful life.

Jon Newsom
Chief, Music Division

The Coolidge Legacy

BY CYRILLA BARR

Of the more than five hundred collections in the Music Division of the Library of Congress a place of primacy must be given to the Elizabeth Sprague Coolidge Collection which was begun in 1924 and whose continuance was ensured by the enlightened act of establishing a trust to support a foundation bearing her name. It was the first such endowment of the Library and as such provided the legal mechanism for creating others over the ensuing years. The uniqueness of her endeavor to involve the U.S. government in the unlikely business of the arts was a bold and original idea that can best be understood through some knowledge of her life before the Library of Congress became the seat of her major philanthropic work.

ELIZABETH SPRAGUE COOLIDGE (1864–1953)

The Making of a Patron

On both sides of her family Elizabeth Sprague Coolidge could trace lineage to colonial times; her father's forebears had come to Salem, Massachusetts, in 1629, her mother's to Plymouth in 1634. Her entry into the realm of philanthropy began in the pre-income-tax period when patronage was most often associated with a politically well-connected and affluent society and was typically a male-dominated arena. Coolidge was in most respects atypical, a parvenu who in time became a vibrant original in the style of her giving. She was a woman in a man's world, was without political party alliance—democratic only in a generic sense—and at most, only modestly affluent if compared with her contemporaries, Vanderbilt, Mellon, Carnegie, and Rockefeller.

Patrons with Coolidge's visionary goals do not spontaneously emerge from nowhere, totally formed as seasoned entrepreneurs. Although she lacked formal education and experience in the world of finance, she had a superb role model in her father, Albert Arnold

Albert Arnold Sprague (1835–1915),
father of Elizabeth Sprague Coolidge.

Nancy Ann Atwood Sprague (1837–1916),
mother of Elizabeth Sprague Coolidge.

Sprague (1835–1915) who, after graduating from Yale in 1849, moved from Vermont to Chicago where he established a successful empire in the wholesale grocery business just as the transcontinental railway was being completed. But it was more than management skills and a sense of fiscal responsibility that Sprague bequeathed to his daughter, for he was also an ardent lover of music and devoted his energies to both Chicago's commercial and its artistic enterprises, serving on the board of many institutions, including the Art Institute of Chicago and the Chicago Symphony. It was from her mother, Nancy Ann Atwood (1837–1916), that Elizabeth inherited her unusual musical talent, for musicmaking was a daily occurrence in the Atwood home, with all of the children performing in some capacity.

The Sprague parental home at 2710 Prairie Avenue, Chicago's "Gold Coast."
The house was designed by the renowned architect Daniel Burnham,
who was Chief of Construction and Director of Works for the
Columbian Exposition in 1893. After the death of her parents,
Elizabeth gave the house to Presbyterian Hospital
to use as a residence for nurses.

Elizabeth Coolidge's activities as a practical musician—performer and composer—set her apart from many patrons and activists of her time. At an early age she began studying piano with Regina (Cohn) Watson who had been a student of Tausig in Germany, and her rapid progress is chronicled in the recital programs of Watson's studio, all carefully preserved in Nancy Sprague's diary. But Elizabeth's dreams of a career were thwarted by the Victorian restraints that prohibited girls of her background and breeding from aspiring to so public a

Elizabeth Sprague Coolidge on her wedding day, November 21, 1891.

Frederic Shurtleff Coolidge (1865–1915), at the time of his marriage to Elizabeth. He was the son of a renowned Boston attorney, David Hill Coolidge, and Isabella Shurtleff, and had just received his MD from Harvard.

life. The struggle was for her all the more acute since two of the most successful female pianists of the period, Teresa Carreño and Fanny Bloomfield-Zeisler, were close friends of the Sprague family. Elizabeth was groomed for matrimony and in 1891 married Frederic Shurtleff Coolidge, a young orthopedic surgeon recently graduated from Harvard: he was the scion of a prominent Boston family whose lineage, like hers, could be traced to colonial times. Although Fred supported and encouraged her musical undertakings, society dictated that she could find outlet for her talents only in the women's clubs of the period.

Despite the privileged life that she enjoyed, Elizabeth, even in her early years, had known adversity and experienced sickness, disappointment, and the death of loved ones. From this period and throughout the remainder of her life Coolidge found solace and consolation in troubled times by immersing herself entirely in her music. It was this early-established habit that sustained her throughout the long and tragic illness of her husband and her own increasing deafness, as she devoted her energies ever more intensely to her musical pursuits. She undertook a serious study of composition working with such respected tutors as Rubin Goldmark, Percy Goetschius, Arthur Whiting, Antonio Brescia, and Daniel Gregory Mason. And even before Frederic's death she established a music school in her home in Pittsfield, Massachusetts, modeled upon the Settlement School of lower east side New York that was administered by her close friends, David and Clara (Damrosch) Mannes.

Between January of 1915 and March of 1916, Coolidge literally lost her entire family; father, mother, and husband died and her only child married and moved away from home. As the sole heir of the estate, she was left without experience or preparation to administer the Sprague fortune, variously reported at some four to five million dollars, plus a personal fund of $200,000. Armed with a keen intellect and formed by the example of her parents, her first philanthropic act in support of music was accomplished with the impressive dispatch and generosity that would become the mark of later beneficence. Just one week after her father's death she established in his name a pension fund for the Chicago Symphony in the amount of $100,000—half of the personal fund that she had just inherited. Without a doubt it was her father's example that had inspired so generous an act, for only days before his sudden death he had established for the employees of the Sprague Warner Company a unique pension fund into which the worker was never required to pay anything. At the time of her mother's death just one year later Coolidge added another $100,000 to the symphony fund.

In the months immediately following this first bequest, she made innumerable gifts not only in support of music, but of medicine as well—memorials to her husband. She gave her

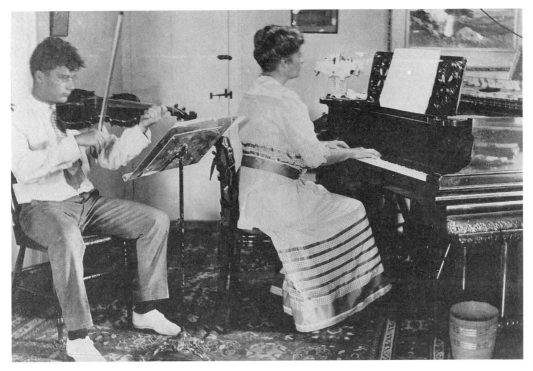

*At her home in Pittsfield, Massachusetts, Elizabeth began a
school in which she took an active part by instructing children in music
herself. Here she is pictured with her son, Sprague, who was a
capable performer on the violin, viola, and oboe.*

home and that of her parents to be used as residences for nurses from two of Chicago's hospitals. In Fred's name she built a hospital for treatment of tuberculosis in Pittsfield, gave her beautiful home there to become the Berkshire Home for Crippled Children, and endowed her cousin Lucy Sprague Mitchell's work in New York that would later become the Bank Street Establishment. Although such swift and generous disposition of money and goods might appear as reckless abandon, for Coolidge it was the "school," the exercise by which she was learning the skills needed to repay her debt to the art that had sustained her through much suffering and hardship, preparing for what she would describe later as her "magnum opus."

The genesis of that great work can be traced to a day in May of 1916 when Coolidge received a letter from a young Austrian violinist, Hugo Kortschak, who had just given up a

Upway Fields, Coolidge's residence in Pittsfield, Massachusetts,
was designed by her brother-in-law Charles Allerton Coolidge.
The home was named Upway after the little village in County Dorset,
England, from which the Spragues came to America in 1628. After her
husband's death in 1915 Elizabeth gave the house to the
Berkshire County School for Crippled Children.

post in the Chicago Symphony in order to dedicate himself to establishing a string quartet. Realizing that the serious pursuit of this ideal required full-time effort and freedom from orchestra commitments for the other three members as well, he appealed to Coolidge to support them while they established themselves, built a repertoire, and polished their style. On the same day that she received Kortschak's appeal she responded in a letter clearly indicating that she had had just such an arrangement in mind for some time. The thought of having her own quartet was undoubtedly inspired by her close friendship with Edward de Coppet and Franz Kneisel, founders of the Flonzaley and Kneisel Quartets.

Within days she went to Chicago to hear Kortschak's quartet and at the audition offered a contract generous enough for all four men to resign their positions in the orchestra and move to the East coast, for a special clause in the contract required the group to be near Coolidge to permit her to perform with them in a repertoire that required piano. The winter months were spent in New York rehearsing in the parlor of her Park Avenue apartment, with her in attendance, score in hand, and the summer in Pittsfield in the Berkshire Mountains, the location that gave the ensemble its name, the Berkshire Quartet.

The Berkshire Experience

While the quartet was building a repertoire, Elizabeth was literally building a home for the quartet, her "Berkshire Boys" as she called them. By 1918 she had constructed, on the slopes of South Mountain just outside of Pittsfield, some small cottages for her musicians and herself, and an auditorium. That same autumn she inaugurated the Berkshire Festival and Berkshire Competition for the composition of chamber music. The festivals were held annually until 1924 and thereafter occurred at irregular intervals. The "Temple," as she called her music hall there, is still the site of summer concerts.

From the outset the Berkshire enterprise was a great success, bringing together from various parts of Europe and America some of the finest musical talents of the period. Even at the first festival in 1918, two months before the Armistice, performers from countries still at war with one another joined to make music in what Coolidge described as "a kind of musical League of Nations."

One of the most important aspects of the Berkshire undertaking was the competition that Coolidge established for the composition of chamber music. The winners received a $1,000 cash prize, and the winning composition was given a performance at the festival by a first-rate ensemble. Even more important was the impetus given to the creation of new

This very formal portrait of Elizabeth, taken in 1902, is just one of many in which her ubiquitous pearls and gloves are to be seen.

chamber music, evidenced by the large number of entries—eighty-two in the first year alone. Blind entries were judged by a jury of distinguished composers and performers carefully selected to include artists well known for their sight-reading abilities, since the procedure included both score study and actual performance of the entries that survived the first and second eliminations. It was Coolidge's belief that all points of view—those of the composer, the performer, and the critic—should be heard.

Over the years the number of entries increased significantly, reaching a high of 257 in 1936, the year of the last competition, and making a grand total of 1,280 since the contest began in 1918. Letters and ledgers identifying the blind entries are part of the Coolidge Collection at the Library of Conress and verify that the unsuccessful contenders included such prominent composers as Hindemith, Křenek, Martinů, Webern, and Zemlinsky, for example.

From the Berkshire Hills to Capitol Hill

Throughout the early years of the Berkshire experience Coolidge was the sole arbiter in the choice of soloists as well as repertoire, and was intimately involved in the general administration of the festival. But with the growth of the enterprise came increasing pressures and inevitable tensions that convinced Coolidge that if her work in support of music were to survive beyond her lifetime it had to be "institutionalized and impersonalized . . . sufficiently important . . . not to be dependent upon the life, the good will, or the bank account of any individual." (*Da Capo, a Paper Read Before the Mother's Club*. [Cambridge, Mass.: 13 March 1951] Washington, DC: Library of Congress, 1952.)

She explored possible affiliations with other institutions; her first offers were to Yale and the American Academy of Arts and Letters. The mere fact that neither accepted did not discourage her, but served to convince her that only a government-administered institution could provide the stability that she sought for her endowment. Such an association was both original and daring and would require an act of Congress to realize it.

It was serendipitous that this moment of decision should coincide with the entry into her life of Carl Engel, the youthful and newly appointed Chief of the Music Division of the Library of Congress, to whom she sent tickets to the fifth Berkshire Festival at the request of their mutual friend Ernest Bloch. Engel was urbane and witty, eager to carry on the work of his predecessor and good friend Oscar Sonneck, and to enlarge the Library's collection. In a simple bread-and-butter letter of 5 October 1922 he thanked Coolidge for sharing with him the cache of manuscripts that she had amassed as a result of her Berkshire competitions and diplomatically ventured to suggest that she might place them with the Library of Congress "as a permanent testimony to the ideals and munificence of a remarkable American woman." A short time later she sent the manuscripts with the suggestion that her Festival Quartet and Elshuco Trio should present a series of concerts at the Library of Congress to bring these works to life in sound.

Engel explained that this could not be done since there was no performance facility in the Library. Indeed all that the Music Division could boast of at this point in time was a rickety old upright piano in the basement. However, within a few months Engel wrote to say that the concerts could take place at the Freer Gallery of Art if she approved. It was an arrangement suggested by and implemented with the help of composer Mary Howe who would later become a good friend of Coolidge. On February 7, 8, and 9, 1924, Coolidge's official association with the Library of Congress was successfully launched with three enthu-

In 1924 when Coolidge suggested sending her Berkshire Quartet to perform at the Library of Congress she could not have known that the only "performing facility" of the Library consisted of an ancient piano in the basement. This photo shows the temporary quarters of the Music Division of the Library of Congress around 1900.

siastically-received concerts that featured six works dedicated to and/or commissioned by her.

A Home for Chamber Music

One of the distinguishing features of Coolidge's patronage was her remarkable ability to undertake several large projects simultaneously; before one good work was accomplished she was already at the drawing board sketching in the details of the next. And so it was that before the elation over the Freer Gallery concerts could subside, she announced her intention to construct an auditorium and to establish an endowment at the Library of Congress. It was her unswerving belief that libraries should not be merely the custodians of manuscripts condemned to preservation as mute artifacts of an earlier time. From the outset it was her desire that this music must be brought to life in performance.

Within days of the Freer Gallery concerts, she communicated to Engel her plans for the "next step" which she promised to share with him viva voce, and which she communicated to Herbert Putnam, Librarian of Congress, in a letter of 23 October 1924. This formal expression of intent, despite its unprecedented vision, created innumerable problems of bureaucratic red tape never before encountered. While there was no problem with the Library accepting material gifts—the manuscripts and the auditorium—no legislation existed permitting it to accept the trust fund, the income of which would be used for operational expenses and the increase of its collection. On the advice of Putnam and with the help of her attorneys, Coolidge submitted a revised version of her letter of intent dated 12 November 1924, which provided only for the donation of the auditorium. On that same day she personally presented to Engel a check for $60,000 for the construction of the building.

By treating the endowment and the auditorium as separate entities Putnam was now able to transmit Coolidge's offer of the building to Congress on 4 December and six days later Sen. George W. Pepper of Pennsylvania introduced the bill in the Senate. After discussion in the Joint Committee on the Library, the bill passed to the House of Representatives where it was introduced by Robert Luce of Massachusetts; it was signed into law by President Coolidge 23 January 1925, just two months after Coolidge's promissory letter. Despite the speed with which this was accomplished, she was impatient with the whole process as was Engel who complained in a letter of 7 January 1925, that "The representatives of our people on Capitol Hill—known collectively as gentlemen from so-and-so, are taking their gentlemanly ease about setting their seal of approval on your wonderful gift."

*In the summer of 1925, during the time that the auditorium
was being built, Coolidge spent several months in Europe while Carl Engel
carefully documented the progress of the building with almost
daily letters to her, and numerous photographs.*

Providing the mechanism for the trust to be accepted would be still more compli-
cated and required further negotiation to circumvent the government's inability to accept
bequests of money. While those legal problems were being disentangled, the construction of
the auditorium began at once. Its progress is extremely well documented in letters since
Coolidge spent the summer in Europe, leaving Engel in complete charge. His letters recount
the progress of the building in great detail and are a testimony to the mutual trust that was
developing between the two. By May Engel could report:

The building is growing visibly. The wooden structure for the ramp is erected. The outline of the stage is discernible. Four steel girders rise to heaven like the legs of a huge upturned animal. The conduits for the lights are laid, the pouring of the concrete has begun. The outer wall is up to the height of the lobby. (Engel to ESC, 21 May 1925)

Coolidge's initial revelation of her intention to build an auditorium unleashed a flood of ebullient letters from Engel revealing that he, like she, had long entertained the desire to make performance a function of the Library. In a note of 29 October 1924 he described his dream of the perfect performing facility for the Library down to the most minute detail. It was his idea to build the auditorium in the courtyard adjoining the Music Division, thus avoiding the cost of purchasing additional land. The use of existing walls would in turn reduce the expense of light, heat and ventilation. By minimizing the cost of the exterior they could then "devote all the available funds to making the interior of the hall just about the most perfect and beautiful room for music that the combined imagination and science of the finest and most competent minds can evolve."

Engel wished to engage John Singer Sargent to decorate the interior of the auditorium with frescoes, but Sargent was ill and would die within that year. Instead Coolidge mandated a "severe and chaste beauty" devoid of "ornate display" that gives the auditorium as we know it today a classic and understated elegance. More importantly, the size and rake of the auditorium, the sight lines, and superb acoustics combine to make it a perfect space for the intimate genre of chamber music. Engel's desire to construct a terrace on the roof of the auditorium, to be decorated with topiary trees from the nearby government botanical garden, did not come to pass either. However, over the next two years the idea would evolve instead into the courtyard that now adjoins the auditorium. Its predominant feature is a pool with cut limestone coping and an interior of faience tile in shades of blue and green. The pool, hedges, topiary trees, and urns with colorful plantings cost a total of $13,775 in 1927.

The Coolidge-Engel correspondence from this period is filled with information concerning the cost of the building, down to such details as the selection of the chairs with their "gray frames and dark green upholstery" at a cost of $11.70 each. Among Engel's more successful achievements for the hall was the installation of a three-manual Skinner organ (since removed). Neither Engel nor Coolidge wanted to commit money from the trust fund for so large an expenditure at this time. Moreover, Coolidge opposed the idea of approaching a donor for the organ, so Engel went directly to the Skinner company with a proposal, hoping to obtain a three-manual organ for under $20,000. By early spring he was pleased to report that:

> Skinner . . . listened with a sympathetic ear to my plea of too many immediate burdens. They are willing to put in the organ without any advance payments. The first payment of $2,500 to be made in January 1926; the same amount the following July. After that $1,500 semi-annually until the $15,500 plus interest are paid. (Engel to ESC, 2 March 1925)

To perpetuate the name of the donor Engel obtained the services of Herbert Putnam's daughter Brenda, a gifted sculptor, to execute Coolidge's profile in a marble bas relief. Money for the installation of the plaque was given by Mary Howe in the name of her children. The bas relief, together with Gary Melchers's portrait of Elizabeth with her four-year-old son Sprague, now graces the foyer of the auditorium—a space that Engel christened as the "sacristy of her Temple."

Elizabeth's favorite recreation was "motoring." Although
she never learned to drive herself, she loved being chauffeured about. Here
she is pictured enjoying her favorite pastime, with two members
of her favorite quartet, the Pro Arte.
On her left is Alphonse Onnou, and on her right, Germain Prévost,
the first violinist and violist of the quartet.

In the letter declaring her intention to build the auditorium Coolidge included a clause allowing that it should "be available (at the discretion of the Librarian and Chief of the Music Division) for any other suitable purpose, secondary to the needs of the Music Division." (ESC to Herbert Putnam, 12 November 1924) At the time she wrote these words she could hardly have imagined the purpose for which it would sometimes be called into service during World War II, but she would likely have been pleased to know that some high-level, clandestine diplomatic meetings between members of Congress and officials of the military were held there. On these occasions staff members of the Music Division resorted to sub rosa passwords such as "General Marshall is giving a concert today" or "The Senate Chorus is being conducted by the Honorable Mr. Barkley."

In its first season the Coolidge Auditorium hosted twenty-five concerts; today more than 20,000 have been heard there. Over the years it has been the venue of performances by such renowned artists as Samuel Barber, Leonard Bernstein, Nadia Boulanger, Nathan Milstein, Gregor Piatigorsky, Leontyne Price, and Artur Rubinstein, as well as nearly every major chamber music organization of this century. Most notable among the string quartets that have performed there are the Pro Arte, London, Gordon, Letz, Coolidge, Kolisch, Rosé, Budapest, and Juilliard. Other ensembles are represented by such diverse groups as the English Singers, the Paris Instrumental Quintet, the Alexander Schneider/Ralph Kirkpatrick Duo, and currently the Beaux Art Trio. In addition, and from the very first, distinguished scholars have lectured there as well—among them Edmund Fellowes, Gustav Holst, Dom Anselm Hughes, and Léon Vallas.

The Eagle Sings

The building of concert halls was not a new experience for Coolidge; the auditorium at the Library of Congress was the third of four that she built in little more than a decade. (The others were Sprague Hall at Yale, 1917; the Temple at South Mountain in Pittsfield, 1918; and Mills College, 1928.) The measure of her detachment and her confidence in Engel is evident from the fact that she sailed to Europe for the summer leaving him to supervise not only the construction of the auditorium, but its dedication as well. Attending to the physical requirements of a beautifully appointed home for chamber music was only part of his job that summer; it also fell to him to realize the plans for the first Library of Congress Festival which would set the precedent for all those to follow.

It was on this occasion that Engel and Coolidge sketched the design of the logo that would thenceforth grace all programs performed in the auditorium—the familiar eagle clutching in its talons not the thunderbolts of war, but Apollo's lyre. Addressing the audience before the first performance Engel referred to the change in the familiar ornithological emblem by declaring that "The eagle has been made to sing." (unpublished typescript, 28 October 1925)

The structure of the Library of Congress Festivals followed the general format that had been tried and proven at the Berkshire Festivals; five concerts spread over three days, beginning with a concert on the afternoon of the first day, with two concerts each on the successive days. The climax of the first festival was planned to coincide with Coolidge's birthday, 30 October, which was designated, and continues to be celebrated, as Founder's Day. In Washington, as in the Berkshires, Coolidge would sponsor competitions and offer commissions. For this first festival she commissioned works by Charles Martin Loeffler, Frederick Stock, and Ildebrando Pizzetti. The main attraction of the initial concert was Loeffler's *Cantico del frate sole*, a medieval Italian text of St. Francis of Assisi, scored for voice and chamber orchestra. It featured the famed Danish soprano Povla Frijsh as soloist.

Although Coolidge wished to be spared details of the business transactions which she delegated to Engel she was, in contrast, a strong voice in such musical matters as the choice of composers and performers. Correspondence from these early years documents the establishment of policies—not the least of which was the question of promoting American music. The issue was vigorously championed by the European-born Engel and initially resisted by seventh-generation-American Coolidge who steadfastly insisted upon programming "the best music," which to her, at least at this point in time, meant European. Their often unvarnished and sharp-witted exchanges reveal that Engel's talents as both critic and shrewd observer of human nature were well matched by Coolidge's astute judgment and keen wit. The verbal sparring that resulted was, in effect, an exercise that increased their mutual respect and trust and in time grew into an enduring friendship. For Coolidge, who jealously guarded the privacy of her personal life, the bestowal of a nickname was always a sign of admission into the privileged inner circle of friends. It is no surprise that early on in their association Engel began to address her as the "Faerie Queene" and she in turn, in a play upon his German name for angel, playfully addressed him as Mike, or the Archangel. A more fanciful invention was Engel's borrowing of the Michelin logo that boasted of its tires that *"il boit l'obstacles."* In their ongoing work with the foundation's business he believed that together they "devoured obstacles," and in a letter of 1928 illustrated the idea with a drawing of two "Michelinesque" figures representing Coolidge and himself, which he playfully inscribed "almost as good as Sargent!" Thereafter they frequently referred to each other as Michel and Line. Although such exchanges may appear to be merely the innocent expressions of a "May and December" friendship, they testify to Engel's importance in the successful launching of Coolidge's partnership with the Library of Congress, an alliance that should not be underestimated.

After the second festival in 1926 the Library of Congress Festivals were not held worried to stay home and leave you, after ... keep and abought a goodbye, these lines will tell you again how happy our meeting up here has made me. I see us now united as an inconquerable pair

← almost as good as Sargent!

" <u>Michel</u> — <u>Line</u> "

... trade mark fits us beautifully. I have just ...nk" <u>two</u> obstacles (for want of something headier), ... was a night-letter to Shober telling him of the

Carl Engel created nicknames for Elizabeth and himself based upon a popular slogan advertising Michelin tires—"we devour obstacles"—which he believed characterized their work. He memorialized it with this drawing of the two of them that is contained in a letter to Elizabeth, August 14, 1926— along with his comment "almost as good as Sargent!"

annually, but alternated with other venues in both Europe and this country. (See "Chronology of Festivals, Competitions, and Commissions.") In 1932 Coolidge inaugurated the Coolidge Medal award on the occasion of Founder's Day. The obverse of the medal was engraved with the logo of the "singing eagle" encircled by the words "Elizabeth Sprague Coolidge Medal for Eminent Services to Chamber Music." The reverse contained the name of the person to whom it was awarded and the date. The Coolidge Medal was inspired by the example of Walter Wilson Cobbett, an Englishman who, like Coolidge, was an amateur musician with a passion for chamber music. In 1924 he began awarding a medal for services to chamber music and in 1925 the second Cobbett medal was given to Elizabeth. Clearly his example was the inspiration for the Coolidge medal, the first of which was awarded to him. Between 1932 and 1948, when the Library discontinued the awarding of such honors, the Coolidge Medal was bestowed upon twenty-five recipients: 1932–Walter Wilson Cobbett, 1933–Adolfo Betti, 1934–Alfredo Casella, 1935–Carl Engel, 1936–Edwin T. Rice, 1937–Gianfrancesco Malipiero, 1938–Frank Bridge, Hugo Kortschak and Jacques Gordon, 1939–Hans Kindler and Alphonse Onnou, 1940–Eugene Goossens and Darius Milhaud, 1941–Randall Thompson, Alexandre Tansman and Benjamin Britten, 1942– Roy Harris and William Kroll, and in 1943–Quincy Porter. No award was made in 1944 when the festival was devoted to celebrating Coolidge's eightieth birthday. The awards resumed in 1945 with Alexander Schneider, 1946–Robert Maas, 1947–Luther Marchant and Louis Speyer, and 1948–Joseph Roisman and Erich Itor Kahn.

Among the more innovative programs mounted in the Coolidge Auditorium were the early excursions into the area of dance. For the third festival in 1928 Coolidge commissioned Igor Stravinsky to compose a pantomime for which she laid out certain parameters to control the length and orchestration. The choice of the subject was the composer's, and the result was *Apollon Musagète* which was conducted by Hans Kindler and choreographed by Adolf Bolm. Although it was not well received by the critics who found it "without coherence, without integrity of style . . . trite, feeble and amorphous" (Lawrence Gilman, *New York Tribune*, 30 April 1928), it was a significant milestone in the career of Stravinsky, for within a year of its premiere *Apollon Musagète* was staged for Diaghilev, marking the beginning of Stravinsky's association with George Balanchine.

Perhaps the best known of all Coolidge's commissions was another ballet, Aaron Copland's *Appalachian Spring,* which was premiered at the tenth Library of Congress Festival in 1944 in celebration of Elizabeth's eightieth birthday. It was one of three ballets commissioned for the occasion; completing the program were Hindemith's *Hérodiade* and Milhaud's *Jeux de Printemps.* All three were choreographed and danced by Martha Graham with a stellar company including Erick Hawkins and Merce Cunningham. As a charming evocation of American frontier life *Appalachian Spring* was an immediate success, capturing a Pulitzer Prize for Copland and winning an enduring place in the hearts of the American public. By bringing together the talents of three prominent composers with the genius of Martha Graham, Coolidge was not merely adding to the ballet repertoire, she was contributing to the maturation of a new dance style. Reflecting on her good fortune and the significance of these new works, Graham wrote to Coolidge in August of 1943 stating her conviction that "American dance has turned a corner, it has come of age."

It is highly unlikely that without the Library of Congress's acceptance of the gift of the auditorium, the Coolidge Foundation would have become a reality—so strong was Coolidge's conviction that music was meant to be enlivened in performance and not merely conserved.

Through the cooperative efforts of Putnam, Engel, and Coolidge's attorney Richard Hale, the problems of establishing the Library of Congress Trust Fund were resolved and the Coolidge Foundation became a reality on 3 March 1925 when President Coolidge signed it into law (Public Law 541, 68th Congress). Elizabeth executed the deed of trust transferring to the Library of Congress the principal of over $400,000 which it was estimated would yield an annual income of $28,000 to be paid quarterly to the benefit of the Music Division. This act officially created the Library of Congress Trust Fund Board consisting of five members: the Secretary of the Treasury (Andrew W. Mellon), the chairman of the Joint Committee on the Library (Senator Fess), the Librarian of Congress (Herbert Putnam), and two persons to be appointed by the president. In consequence of this action the Library was now empowered to accept other possible trusts in the future. The purpose and function of the Coolidge Foundation are clearly spelled out in the document: its primary aim was to aid the Music Division in the development of the study, composition, and appreciation of music by enabling it to

> *conduct periodic festivals,*
> *give concerts and defray the expenses thereof,*
> *offer and award prizes for original compositions,*
> *pay an honorarium to the Chief and,*
> *further the cause of musicology.*

The awards ceased after a furor was created when one was bestowed upon Ezra Pound, and the Chief of the Music Division was no longer paid an honorarium when it was discovered that this made his salary greater than that of the Librarian of Congress.

Lastly Coolidge provided a statement empowering the Board "to do any and all other lawful acts and things designed to promote the art of music, so far as any of the foregoing purposes come within the charitable uses which are allowed and can be sustained by law, this proviso being inserted out of caution, to make the public and charitable purpose of this gift unambiguous and unmistakable." (*Report of the Librarian of Congress*, 1925, p. 4.)

Since the bequest of the auditorium and establishment of the foundation occurred during Calvin Coolidge's administration it is not surprising that Elizabeth was often mistakenly identified as the wife of the president. Composer and friend Frank Bridge was fond of sending to her erroneous notices in the British press such as this one from the *London Daily Mirror*:

> I wonder how many people present at the opening of the Diaghileff season at His Majesty's Theatre knew that Stravinsky's *Apollo* [sic] *musagète* which is included in the program, was commissioned by Mrs. Calvin Coolidge, wife of the American President. Mrs. Coolidge has always been tremendously fond of music, but the "silent" president lives up to his name by choosing movies as his form of entertainment. (Frank Bridge to ESC, 26 June 1928)

Elizabeth was amused by such mistakes and good-naturedly responded by identifying herself simply as "the other Mrs. Coolidge."

Foundation Outreach

Unlike the Freer Gallery concerts that had consisted almost entirely of modern composi-tions, the inaugural concert in the Coolidge Auditorium cautiously framed the contempo-rary works of Loeffler, Stock, and Jacobi between a Bach chorale at the opening and a Handel organ concerto at the close of the program. Nonetheless, critics complained of "too much modernity" and found much of the music "devoid of form and harmony," having "passages of some beauty which but emphasized the many measures of riotous noises." Although Richard Aldrich, critic of the *New York Times*, described Washington as "one of the most unmusical capitals of the world," Elizabeth was not discouraged. The rather uncom-prehending response to her musical offering only convinced her to devote herself to a con-scious effort at audience education.

Because the Coolidge Auditorium was located in the nation's capital and in a gov-ernment agency, certain courtesies were required by diplomatic protocol, hence invitations were issued for the first festival. Beyond that, the social register meant nothing to Coolidge. From the outset she had made it very clear that the concerts she supported were always to be free and open to the general public. But when the size of the popular audience clamor-ing for entrance far exceeded the capacity of the hall's 511 seats Engel resorted to requiring a ticket to be procured in advance from a local concert bureau in downtown Washington at the cost of twenty-five cents. Coolidge objected on principle to even this modest charge. Engel's action was motivated in part by his fear that without some control the concerts sponsored by the Foundation might unwittingly be catering to an elitist group, thus having a purely social influence. By requiring tickets he believed that "the low price would enable anyone to come and would not deter the real music lovers from among our 'swells,' but rather turn away those 'swells' who now clamor for admission because they think the concerts fashionable."

In time the system reverted to Coolidge's original intention and to this day free admission is on a "first come first served" basis in keeping with the belief that "nothing should be too good for the common man, and he should be the first to know how good it is." (Engel to ESC, 23 March 1928)

From the very beginning Coolidge envisioned her foundation as the means to reach a much larger audience by sponsoring concerts in colleges, universities and public libraries all across the country. She began by obtaining additional performances for the European artists that she engaged as a way of helping to defray their expenses. It was actually a logical outgrowth of the festivals she sponsored at the Library of Congress, for by this means Coolidge was turning what would otherwise have been merely a one-time appearance into multiple engagements, creating opportunities for the artists and at the same time reaching a far greater audience. She did, however, establish the policy that the American debut of her artists must be at the Library of Congress and under her auspices; thereafter they could perform anywhere. Among the many notable European artists who were introduced to American audiences through Coolidge's efforts were Myra Hess, Rudolf Serkin, Adolph Bush, the English Singers, the London String Quartet, and the Pro Arte Quartet of Brussels. Coolidge's policy of extension concerts yielded benefits for the host institution as well, since the Foundation paid half the fee of the performers. For the artists it meant a wider public and for the contemporary composers whose works were being performed it provided a greater exposure for their music.

In some years there was no festival either in the Berkshires or at the Library of Congress. In 1927 and 1931, for example, she sponsored extensive European tours and in 1930 she staged a lavish festival in her hometown of Chicago. The Chicago event is especially significant since it marked the beginning of her long association with Hindemith who received his first Coolidge commission on this occasion. The other major commissions that would follow over the years, and the friendship that developed between the two were, by his own admission, factors influential in his eventual move to the United States.

Even before her association with the Library of Congress, Coolidge had begun to sponsor music in Europe, and in the late 1920s and early 1930s she funded extensive tours in twenty-one cities of ten different countries: London, Cambridge, Oxford, Amsterdam, Bruges, Brussels, Ghent, Liege, Louvain, Paris, Graz, Vienna, Frankfurt, Berlin, Rome,

With the outbreak of World War II, Coolidge was forced
to discontinue her festivals in Europe and simply changed the venues to
Mexico, Puerto Rico, and Hawaii. Here she is seen chatting with
William Kroll at a luau celebrating her 1939 Honolulu Festival.

Naples, Venice, Asolo, Moscow, Prague, and Budapest. For these tours she commissioned new works and paid all performance-related expenses, as well as the travel and maintenance of the composers and performers in her entourage—for she always traveled with them. The incredible example of this American woman sponsoring free concerts in a foreign country and for people she had never met, earned for her the title of "the American Maecenas." However, in the troubled years preceding the outbreak of World War II Coolidge ceased her European festivals and simply moved the venue to Mexico City, Honolulu, and San Juan.

Radio Work

Coolidge's excursion into the area of radio broadcasting must certainly be considered one of her most innovative and successful endeavors. Despite the opposition of some of her most trusted advisors she insisted that her new auditorium be equipped to broadcast; thus the inaugural festival in 1925 was carried over the airwaves by the 1,000-watt Navy Telephone Station, NAA, in Arlington, Virginia. The attempt was commendable but the results poor, in part because the broadcasts were at a time and on a wave length that interfered with other stations. Nonetheless, the experiment aroused the interest of the networks and soon Coolidge's programs were being carried by the Columbia, National, and Mutual Broadcasting Companies. In the 1934–1935 season alone she sponsored nineteen broadcasts. The fact that her initial efforts predated by two years the establishment of the Federal Radio Commission of 1927 (precursor of the Federal Communications Commission of 1934) underscores her remarkable vision. Her prescient conviction of the educational potential of radio as a tool of audience education is clearly spelled out in an address which she gave to the American Federation of Music Clubs. (undated typescript ms., Coolidge Collection, LC) It is clear from her words that she saw radio as indispensable to her goal of enhancing

> the cultural development and the enlargement of the American audience. Only by meeting its message can Art fulfill its vivifying function. The listener is as vitally necessary to its organic growth and health as is the composer; therefore, my aim has been to increase the number of such listeners and to multiply their opportunities for such listening, both locally and by radio.

In an address to her radio audience, 8 January 1934, on the occasion of the inaugural broadcast of her NBC cycle, she voiced her conviction that "practically everyone loves chamber music who understands it; and . . . almost everyone understands it who hears it enough."

She again addressed her radio public at the opening of her 1936 chamber music series carried by the National Broadcasting Company. This time her message was one of satisfaction in the victory over the doubts and misgivings that first confronted her "insistent and obstinate idea of broadcasting *to* the largest possible audience, *by* the best possible performers *of* the best possible music; and of doing this freely and frequently until we cannot live without it." Privately she confided to Carolyn Cushing (4 March 1936) "I have never done anything that gave me more personal satisfaction and, of course, that is a hundred-fold greater (perhaps I might almost say a million-fold because they tell me that these broadcasts reach millions of listeners) on account of being able to share it so widely."

Her relationship with the networks was not, however, without its problems. She frequently chastised them for truncating pieces to fit into rigid time slots, and complained bitterly of their growing commercialism. But these disagreements were more than compensated by the enthusiastic letters received from grateful listeners in the musical hinterlands,

In her later years, Elizabeth's grandchildren were the light of her life. Here she is seen reading The Wind in the Willows *to the twins, John and Fred, and her namesake Elizabeth.*

such as this one from a British airman on mess duty in a remote Canadian outpost who heard her Sunday morning broadcasts of organist E. Power Biggs. "Your program reaches us at 6:15 a.m. Sometimes . . . that hour finds me . . . frying eggs and bacon by the hundreds over colossal hot stoves while your music drifts in like something from another world." (Carlisle Estes to E. Power Biggs, 11 November 1943)

Even a cursory examination of programs that Coolidge sponsored over the years testifies to the effectiveness of her crusade to create a musically literate audience for chamber music. Only a few years after the uncomprehending audience of the first festival found Debussy's Quartet "chaotic" Coolidge was commissioning and programming some of the most avant-garde works of the period. In 1933, for example, she sponsored the Pro Arte Quartet in a program devoted exclusively to Schoenberg. Nor did she exempt herself from the task of understanding the contemporary.

Elizabeth was seventy-two years old when Jerzy Fitelberg's Fourth Quartet won the Coolidge prize in 1936. She wrote to a friend, "I confess that his idiom is as yet too strange to me to enable me to understand his work: therefore, I have not yet really enjoyed it. But I have recently received the score which I intend to study in the hope of being able to respond to his work." (ESC to David Ussher, 22 April 1937)

Although Coolidge always continued to sponsor performances of the standard repertoire, she was a militant crusader for the cause of contemporary music, and maintained a healthy detachment from the works that were generated through her commissions. It mattered little if she liked them; she recognized the importance of extending the boundaries of musical knowledge. She made that point emphatically in her address to the National Federation of Music Clubs. "My plea for modern music is not that we should like it, nor necessarily that we should even understand it, but that we should exhibit it as a significant human document."

With the establishment of the Coolidge Foundation Program for Contemporary Chamber Music, the Library began a new and experimental venture intended to broaden the repertoire of performing ensembles in the United States. Through this agency professional groups—defined as "those in residence at academic institutions, and faculty groups that meet regularly and perform together as a part of their academic activities"—were encouraged to draw upon a special loan collection of contemporary music chosen by the Selection Committee of the Coolidge Foundation. A list of the available works was provided and the borrowing ensembles were entitled to select up to six compositions which could be retained for one month. Scores, parts and, when possible, recordings of the works were available free of charge. It was the expressed desire of the Foundation that "many of the works borrowed will excite the interest of the ensembles and encourage them to acquire these compositions for their libraries and for frequent public performance." (Checklist of works available, 3rd supplement, 1967)

Musicological Activities

One of Coolidge's least well-known benefactions was her support of musicological endeavors. Within only days of the dedication of the auditorium the first series of historical lectures was offered by Edmund Fellowes and in the succeeding years an impressive list of scholars have been heard there. And in the period between the two world wars her contributions assisted Guido Adler to carry on with publication of the *Denkmäler der Tonkunst in Österreich*. In return for her support of Carl Geiringer he dedicated to her the first edition of his biography of Haydn.

Coolidge had a keen interest in early music and it was perhaps that, along with her great personal friendship for Gian Francesco Malipiero, that prompted her to underwrite his editions of the *Opera Omnia* of Monteverdi and Vivaldi. Her support of the Lully edition of Henry Prunières was cut short by his death in 1942.

Of all her efforts for the cause of musicology perhaps the most forward looking was her attempt to establish, as a memorial to Oscar Sonneck, a scholarship for the study of American music at a time when Americans were still trudging off to Europe to study and long before musicologists were at all serious about investigating our own country's music. Interestingly enough, this visionary project was her only unsuccessful enterprise ever. It was a noble idea born before its time, but after several years of actually not being able to give the money away she reluctantly admitted defeat.

The Coolidge Collection

The prize-winning manuscripts from the Berkshire competition that Coolidge gave to the Library of Congress in 1924 are the nucleus of what in time would become the vast Coolidge Collection, comprising scores, correspondence, personal memorabilia, original art works, and assorted gifts.

Scores

Over the years the Coolidge Foundation has been responsible for some of the most important commissions of the twentieth century—works that were seminal not only within the canon of the individual composer—but in the development of chamber music in general. After Coolidge's death Harold Spivacke, then Chief of the Music Division, wrote to Anna Malipiero (26 January 1954), "We know only definitely the works which were commissioned by the Coolidge Foundation. Strange as it may sound we have only a vague notion of Mrs. Coolidge's personal commissions since she did not keep any record of them."

Although she was at times surprisingly casual in this matter, Coolidge was very specific about performance rights of the works she commissioned through the Foundation. In most cases the contract provided for exclusive performance (for North America only) during a period of six months from the date of the first performance and without payment for the use of the orchestral materials. The Library of Congress was to have the world premiere of the work and the autograph manuscript was to remain in the Library's collection, with the understanding that it should not be copied.

It is impossible to know just how many of the manuscripts that Coolidge deposited are actually the result of personal commissions offered outside the purview of the Foundation. The compilation provided herein is based upon information culled from the correspondence, dedications indicated on the manuscripts themselves, and the official list of Coolidge Foundation Commissions. (See "Commissions, Dedications, and Prize-Winning Compositions.") It is at best an approximation and does not include the hundreds of works that were unsolicited gifts presented, very possibly, in the hope of gaining the favor of a commission. Such works were often accompanied by unreasonable requests and became both a problem and a source of irritation to Coolidge. As early as 1930 she wrote to Carl Engel:

> The business of receiving manuscripts and testimonials with flowery letters of dedication is becoming a veritable burden to me, especially as with these offerings usually goes an expectation of sponsorship . . . on my part, and if these are not forthcoming within the expected time, I am held responsible, blamed, and sometimes curtly requested to return the manuscripts. I am at a loss to know just how to deal with this phase of my career. (26 September 1930)

Many manuscripts, however, were genuine expressions of gratitude from such friends as Bridge and Malipiero who had already been the recipients of her support and who in time gave her additional works as outright gifts with no strings attached. Taken together the scores—commissions, prize winners, dedications and assorted gifts—total approximately three hundred works and constitute a significant contribution to the Library's collection of contemporary compositions. In addition Coolidge assisted with the purchase of some outstanding twentieth-century works. In 1934, for example, when Berg was in desperate financial need he approached Engel with an offer to sell the holograph of *Wozzeck*, but the Library was unable to meet the asking price of 6,000 Austrian shillings (about $1,040 at the time). Engel was able to obtain about $600 from the Friends of Music, and Coolidge supplied the remainder from her own funds.

And finally, it is important to recognize the vast number of compositions, collections of private papers, and miscellanea that others have given to the Library through Coolidge's

Harold Spivacke, who became Chief of the Music Division of
the Library of Congress in 1937, was a genial partner and good friend of Coolidge.
In her declining years he did much to shield her from the routine
red tape and tensions that were bound to arise in their work. Much of the
credit for the realization of Appalachian Spring, *undoubtedly*
Coolidge's best-known commission, should go to Spivacke
who worked behind the scenes to bring the ballet to fruition.

influence. Although these are not actually a part of the Coolidge Collection as such, they are bequests from friends and associates of hers—many of them recipients of her benefactions—who were influenced by her friendship, her example, and her close association with the Library. Some of the most significant are the bequests of Mario Castelnuovo-Tedesco, Alexander Schneider, and Aaron Copland, for example.

Coolidge's Compositions

At various times in her life, Coolidge devoted serious efforts to the study of composition, especially during the time of her husband's devastating illness and again when in her last years her hearing was so impaired that she could no longer enjoy performing herself. That she had no illusions about her skills as a composer is evident from a letter she wrote to her investment broker who at the time of the Library of Congress endowment feared that she might be financially overextended. She responded that she had just received a royalty check for $9.99 and assured him, "You see, I shall never have to worry about money." Nonetheless, she undertook her composing with that same seriousness that characterized everything that she did. This is evident from the many reams of manuscript paper filled with her composition exercises, as well as from her teachers' remarks in her assignment notebooks, all contained in the Coolidge Collection. The greater share of her music is for voice; much of which was written for children—two early collections for her son and later a set for each grandchild. Her most ambitious undertaking is the Browning Cycle (1901) of ten songs based upon the Sonnets of Elizabeth Barrett Browning. For this and several other works she later supplied string quartet accompaniment. Her instrumental works include a string quartet (ca. 1915) that was actually recorded by the Manhattan String Quartet in 1933, a Piano Trio in F Major (1930), and a Sonata for Oboe and Piano (1947) written for her son, Sprague, who was an accomplished oboist and violist.

In 1916 Frederick Stock requested Coolidge's permission to arrange the first two movements of her string quartet for full string orchestra. Under his direction they were performed by the Chicago Symphony Orchestra as a memorial to Elizabeth's mother and father in whose memory she had endowed the Orchestra's pension fund. Stock's arrangements are part of the Coolidge Collection of scores.

The Coolidge Bequest

Patronage in one form or another has existed throughout history from antiquity to the present, from Maecenas to the National Endowment for the Arts. But the function of the individual aristocratic patron within a democratic society raises some important and very timely questions. Of the various solutions demonstrated in this century perhaps none is so innovative as that of Coolidge, and none speaks so eloquently to the present need for private support of the arts.

In the early 1900s industrialists like Carnegie, Ford, and Rockefeller amassed fortunes so great that even conspicuous consumption was not adequate to the task of disposing of surplus wealth. This would be somewhat altered with the ratification of the sixteenth amendment to the Constitution in 1913 that created the institution of income tax. The coming together of two forces in American life—large fortunes and the development of arts management groups which functioned like business—resulted in the rise of foundations which have since become the servant of philanthropy.

It was in this era that Mrs. Coolidge entered the arena of the philanthropist, a solitary woman with neither preparation nor experience. Her fortune was certainly not of the same magnitude as the wealth of the giant industrialists. The Vanderbilts at this time possessed more money than some sovereign states, and in one year alone Andrew Carnegie gave more than six million dollars for the restoration and purchase of organs and pianos. Coolidge's entire inheritance was considerably less than that amount but, thanks to her very astute management and her extraordinarily single-minded devotion to a cause, she was able to establish her patronage on a sound financial basis that continues to this day to enhance American musical life.

Two elements in particular mark the unique style of her giving. First of all, she did not believe in the dole. While she was extraordinarily generous, she could be almost parimonious when she believed she was being exploited. She was endowed with an uncanny ability to discern the blandishments of opportunists from the appeals of the genuinely deserving. Nothing rankled her Yankee conviction of the value of hard work more than outright requests for money—especially when these came from people she did not know—and she could be severe in her admonitions against them. Her personal life was an example, for she never succumbed to indulgence in her own lifestyle or to the tasteless ostentation that often characterizes the nouveaux riches. Hers was instead a deeply ingrained work ethic founded on the conviction that the enjoyment of comforts and privileges resulting from wealth should only serve to dictate a greater awareness of morality in the stewardship of that wealth.

By her astute management of money and her intimate involvement in her endowments she created a method of giving that was designed to indoctrinate the recipient in the art of sound fiscal planning. She literally trained others in the art of philanthropic giving by instituting a program and then gradually withdrawing support over a period of years, until the project was either being supported by others—usually recruited by her—or had become self-sufficient. She always required some service in return for her support, usually in the form of teaching, giving free concerts, or assuming the organization of her European tours. Out of such arrangements grew the concept of "Artist-in-Residence," the first example being the Pro Arte Quartet at the University of Wisconsin, an affiliation that continues to this day.

The second quality of Coolidge's patronage which sets it apart from that of others, such as Isabella Stuart Gardner, for example, is that she was herself a musician. Her nearly exclusive dedication to chamber music is in part due to her desire to be able to perform with the ensembles that she supported. Moreover, common sense dictated that she could simply do more with less money by patronizing smaller performing organizations, a fact that also allowed for greater control than she would have had over symphonic or operatic ventures.

Throughout Coolidge's correspondence there is a repeated call for "loyalty to standards" which translates not only as upholding high standards of musical performance, but also exactitude in maintaining records, responding to letters and paying bills. Not even the most insignificant error or indiscretion seemed to escape her. But she exacted this same high standard of conduct from herself as well.

While her concept of philanthropy was visionary her exercise of it was eminently practical. Much of her success must be attributed to the fact that her work was built upon the solid bedrock of her unwavering belief in what she did. This is clearly articulated in her address to the National Federation of Music Clubs:

> My desire is to serve Art, and through Art, to serve humanity . . .for I feel that the survival of the human spirit largely depends upon its artistic freedom: to lose the privilege of self expression by which, through his Art . . . man has recorded Truth and Beauty, would be to limit spiritual nourishment . . . [W]hat I have tried to do for my composers and their audiences may ultimately result in a reaction which shall be beneficial to the whole world of music—creative, executive, critical and even managerial; for indeed I think we are today in pitiful need of its tonic and healing support.

Fundamental to Coolidge's philosophy was her unswerving conviction that philanthropy should not be viewed as the exclusive domain of the very rich, and she successsfully demonstrated that principle by singlehandedly creating a mechanism by which a modest fortune continues to enrich the lives of many. Her contribution to the Library of Congress became the "mustard seed," from whose example 150 such endowments have sprouted and grown, over twenty of them in the Music Division alone.

Elizabeth Sprague Coolidge stands as an example and role model for our own time. Her unerring practical sense would not allow her to believe that her work was ever complete. The lesson she taught, and the legacy she left us are a challenge that is eloquently expressed in her own words:

My faith in altruistic cooperation is strong, as is my belief in the civilizing discipline of culture. But we must put it to the test first, mustn't we? For, alas, altruism is of slow growth, and requires patience and forbearance, sometimes obstinacy. With all these to hope for what may we not achieve? (ESC to Aurelio Henry Reinhardt, President of Mills College, August 10, 1933)

Musical Compositions by Elizabeth Sprague Coolidge

Vocal Works

After Supper Songs (voice and piano)
Chicago: H.S. Stone, 1899

Echoes (voice and piano)
Poetry by Thomas More
G. Schirmer, 1904

Fifteen Mother Goose Melodies (voice and piano)
G. Schirmer, 1904

Four Songs for Elizabeth (voice and piano)
   Over the Meadow
   The Wind
   As I Was Going Along
   There Was a Little Girl
Holograph, 19??

Four Songs for Fred (voice and piano)
   Billy Boy
   Tweedledum and Tweedledee
   When Little Fred
   The House that Jack Built
Pencil and ink, 1921

Four Songs for John (voice and piano)
    The Kitten's Quartet
    Rain, Rain, Go Away
    Ride Away, Ride Away
    Little Brown Brother
Pencil and ink, 19??

Infant Joy (high voice and piano)
Holograph, 19??

Laughing Song (medium voice and piano)
From William Blake's "Songs of Innocence"
Ink and pencil, 19??

O Babe of Joy (voice and piano)
Text and music, ESC
Dedicated to baby Elizabeth
Holograph, 1921

O My Luv's Like a Red, Red Rose (medium voice and piano)
Holograph, 1904

Slumber Songs of the Madonna (medium voice and piano)
Texts by Alfred Noyes
Holograph, 1915

Slumber Songs of the Madonna (medium high voice with piano)
    See, What a Wonderful Smile
    Clenched Little Hands
    G. Schirmer, 1920

Slumber Songs of the Madonna
Revised version with oboe obbligato, 1935
    Sleep, Little Baby, I Love Thee
    Is It a Dream?
    See, What a Wonderful Smile!
    For in the Warm Blue Summer Weather

Clenched Little Hands
But Now You Are Mine

Sonnets: A Cycle of Browning Songs (high voice and piano)
Dedicated to Frederic Shurtleff Coolidge, 12 November 1901
   I Saw in Vision, Through My Tears
   Unlike Are We, Unlike Our Destinies
   A Heavy Heart, Beloved, Have I Borne!
   And Yet Because Thou Overcomest So
   The Face of All the World Is Changed, I Think
   If Thou Must Love Me Let It Be for Love's Sake Only
   Over Again, Yet Over Again
   When Our Two Souls Stand Up Erect and Tall
   Thy Soul Hath Snatched Up Mine
   How Do I Love Thee?

Sonnets: Cycle of Songs, being inspired by and adapted from
"Sonnets from the Portuguese"
by Elizabeth Barrett Browning (arranged for string quartet).

SONGS FOR THREE OR MORE VOICES

Christmas Sextet for Family
   Six voices, violin, viola, violoncello, clarinet and four-hand piano
Holograph, 1929

How Does my lady's Garden Grow? (trio for women's voices)
Holograph, 19??

Peter Piper (three-voiced canon with optional piano)
Inscribed to Sprague
Holograph, 1928

Instrumental Music

String Quartet in E Minor
Holograph, 191?

Largo Lamentoso and Scherzo
from the Quartet in E Minor, arranged for String Orchestra by
Frederck Stock. As played by the Chicago Symphony, 3 February
1916 as a memorial to Albert Arnold Sprague.
Inscribed "To the composer of this Fine Music with all
Good Wishes."

Trio in F Major
Score and parts
Partly holograph, partly copyists manuscript, 1930

Sonata for Oboe and Piano
Carl Fischer, 1947

Correspondence

In many respects the correspondence, measured at 16 linear meters, is the heart of the Coolidge Collection for it illuminates—often in surprisingly candid detail—the circumstances and exchanges that brought the musical creations into existence, as well as the difficulties of dealing with composers who were dilatory in fulfilling their commissions. While she was respectful of those with whom she worked Coolidge was never star struck and did not hesitate to express her disappointment when composers and artists, no matter how famous they might be, failed to meet their obligations on time. On occasion not even the great and famous escaped her rebukes. When at the end of 1925 Ravel had not yet delivered his Chansons Madécasses she dispatched Prunières with instructions to "tell Mr. Ravel that I am greatly disappointed as the time goes by and he does not fulfill his promise of sending me the other two songs which were positively promised by the first of January and for all three of which I have already paid him." (ESC to Henry Prunières, 28 December 1925)

The collection contains several thousand letters and telegrams that not only document the policies, finance, and inner workings of the Coolidge Foundation, but also reveal a good deal about her personality. Her amazonian stature and forthright manner of conducting her business affairs notwithstanding, Coolidge could be genuinely tender and compassionate as her letters to close friends often testify. This is particularly true of her preoccupation with the safety of her European friends who were in serious danger during World War II.

A book could be written about her assistance to European composers and performers attempting to escape from persecution in the 1930s, whether for reasons of race, religion, or political and ideological conflict. Some important compositions resulted from commissions offered to displaced composers, and many of the refugees obtained positions in educational institutions and symphony orchestras through her influence. In one instance, as in the case of Darius Milhaud who obtained a position at Mills College in Oakland through her intercession, she actually assisted the college by paying a substantial portion of his salary.

It is clear that on occasion Coolidge allowed herself to abandon formality and engage in more familiar exchanges—even with some of her most famous correspondents, such as when she and Prokofiev commiserated over their respective dental problems. Her witty and sometimes ascerbic assessments of problems with temperamental performers are often delivered in a prose style that would be the envy of many a writer, yet she resisted all admonitions of those who encouraged her to write her autobiography. And not even Carl Engel could convince her to allow her letters to be published. He reluctantly agreed and had to admit that "some of your most pertinent and humanly interesting remarks [would] have to be left out, because of references too frank—if only too just—to living persons. What should give spice and zest to these letters are precisely such passages that it would be a shame to omit." (Engel to ESC 24 May 1937)

Coolidge's correspondence is an invaluable repository of material essential to the history of twentieth-century music in general and of chamber music in particular.

Memorabilia

Among the memorabilia are numerous clippings, photographs, diaries, scrapbooks, autograph albums, essays, paintings, and composition exercises—some of which date from her early life. The citations and academic hoods are a reminder of the accolades that began to accumulate as her work became known around the globe. She was awarded honorary degrees from Mount Holyoke (1926), Smith College (1927), Yale (1927), Mills College (1928), the University of California (1933), and Pamona (1938). For her work in Europe, Coolidge was recognized by the bestowal of various honors from foreign governments. In 1931 she was inducted as a Chevalier of France's Legion of Honor, and was presented with the key to the city of Frankfurt. In 1935 she was awarded the Order of the Crown of Belgium and the medal *Hommage de gratitude* from the University of Liège, and in 1937 was honored with the bestowal of the Order of Léopold, King of Belgium. There is little in her correspondence however to suggest that, except for the Legion of Honor (for which she

*In 1923 Coolidge attempted to engage John Singer Sargent
to paint her portrait. He responded that he was no longer able to undertake
large works in oil but would be happy to do this charcoal portrait
of her which is now part of the Library of Congress collection.*

was nominated by poet Paul Claudel), she gave particular notice to these honors and decorations.

There are various other gifts among the Coolidge memorabilia but perhaps none so important to her personally as the remembrances of the famous concert that she sponsored in 1929 for the reclusive Gabriele d'Annunzio at his villa on Lake Garda. Here the Italian government maintained him in resplendent—albeit powerless—isolation. He met Coolidge and her party with a twenty-one-gun salute from the canon mounted on the deck of the battleship that he had requested the government to reconstruct for him in his garden. Delighted by the concert in his honor d'Annunzio presented each of the guests with a gift fashioned by his personal jeweler. To Coolidge he gave a silver cigarette case mounted with a carved opal cameo with the head of an American Indian. The cigarettes still remain inside.

Original Art Works

Beside the bas relief by Brenda Putnam and Gari Melchers's portrait of Coolidge with her four-year-old son Sprague—both located in the foyer of the auditorium—there are two other important original works of art. The first is a bronze bust of Coolidge done by Jo Davidson in 1934 and given to the Library in the name of Coolidge's son Sprague. The other is a portrait of her by John Singer Sargent dating from 1921. She had requested it to be done in oil but Sargent responded that his health was failing and he could no longer undertake such a demanding work, but would instead be happy to do something in a less labor-intensive medium. The result is an extraordinarily beautiful portrait of Coolidge done in charcoal.

Chronology of Festivals, Competitions, and Commissions

YEAR	BERKSHIRE	LIBRARY OF CONGRESS	AWARDEE	COMMISSION
1918	1st		Tadeusz Iarecki	
1919	2nd		Ernest Bloch	
1920	3rd		G. F. Malipiero	
1921	4th		H. Waldo Warner	
1922	5th		Leo Weiner	
1923	6th			Rebecca Clarke
				Eugene Goossens
1924	7th		Wallingford Riegger	
1925		1st		Ch. M. Loeffler
				Frederick Stock
				Ildebrando Pizzetti
1926		2nd	Albert Huybrechts	
1927				
1928	8th	3rd		Igor Stravinsky
1929		4th	Joseph Hüttel	
1930				
1931	5th			
1932			Bohuslav Martinů	
1933		6th		
1934	9th			
1935		7th		
1936			Jerzy Fitelberg	

YEAR	BERKSHIRE	LIBRARY OF CONGRESS	AWARDEE	COMMISSION
1937		8th		
1938	10th			
1939				
1940		9th		
1944		10th		Aaron Copland
				Paul Hindemith
				Darius Milhaud
1950		11th		
1953				Samuel Barber
1956		12th		Gian-Carlo Menotti
				Luigi Dallapiccola
1964		13th		Luigi Dallapiccola
				Alberto Ginastera
				Howard Hanson
				Giselher Klebe
				G. F. Malipiero
				Riccardo Malipiero
				Darius Milhaud
				Aurelia de la Vega
				William Schuman
1970		14th		Milton Babbitt
				George Crumb
				Luigi Dallapiccola
				Jean-Claude Eloy
				Cristobal Halffter
				Juan Orrego-Salas
				Mel Powell
1975		15th		Hugh Aitken

NB: For a complete listing of commissions, see *"Commissions, Dedications, and Prize-Winning Compositions."*

Commissions, Dedications, and Prize-Winning Compositions

This compilation is based upon various partial lists of Coolidge's personal commissions, information culled from the correspondence, dedications indicated on the manuscripts themselves, and the official list of Coolidge Foundation commissions. It is at best an approximation. Nearly all works commissioned up to the time of Coolidge's death in 1953 were also dedicated to her. In addition it is likely that many of the works here indicated solely as dedications were actually also personal commissions, for Mrs. Coolidge was, especially in the early years, surprisingly casual about keeping a record of her commissions.

LEGEND:

ESC	COMMISSIONS OFFERED PERSONALLY	BPhm	BERKSHIRE PRIZE, HONORABLE MENTION
CF	COOLIDGE FOUNDATION COMMISSION	PFhm	PAN AMERICAN FESTIVAL, HONORABLE MENTION
CP	COOLIDGE PRIZE	G	GIFT
BP	BERKSHIRE PRIZE	D	DEDICATION

COMPOSER	TITLE	DATE	CATEGORY
Aitken, Hugh	**Fables: A Diversion for Soprano, Two Tenors and Bass,** With flute, two oboes, bassoon and string quartet	1974	CF
Alfano, Franco	**Per Santa Elizabetta**	1931	D
	Sonata for Violoncello and Piano	1926	D
Arma, Paul	**Concerto for String Quartet**	1948?	D
Babbitt, Milton	**String Quartet No. 4**	1970	CF
Balassa, Sandor	**A Daydreamer's Diary, Op. 35**	1983	CF
Barati, George	**String Quartet**	1944	D
Barber, Samuel	**Hermit Songs**	1953	CF
Bartók, Béla	**String Quartet No. 5**	1934	CF
Bartolucci, Ernesto	**String Quartet in A, Op. 25**	1945	D
Bax, Arnold	**Legend for Violin and Piano**	n.d.	D
	Octet for Horn, Strings, and Piano	1934	D
	Sextet for Horn, Strings, and Piano	1964	G

COMPOSER	TITLE	DATE	CATEGORY
Beck, Conrad	Concerto for String Quartet and Orchestra	1929	D
Bedford, Herbert	Lyrical Interlude: Pathways of the Moon	1929	D
	For flute, oboe, violin, piano		
Bercerra, Gustavo	Piano Quintet	1962	CF
Berezowsky, Nicolai	Sextet, Op. 26, for Three Violins, Two Violas, and		
	Violoncello	1940	CF
	Theme and Fantastic Variation, Op. 7	n.d.	D
Bergsma, William	Concerto for Wind Quintet	1958	CF
Bettingen, Balthasar	Concerto for Viola da Gamba and Orchestra	1931	G
Beveridge, Thomas	Serenade	1978	CF
Bliss, Arthur	Music for Oboe and Four Strings	1927	CF
	String Quartet	1941	G
Bloch, Ernest	Suite for Viola and Piano	1919	BP
Bossi, Renzo	Trio in 4 tempi concatenati in do maggiore	1921	BPhm
Brescia, Domenico	Ricercare and Fugue for Organ	1931	D
	Suite for Flute, Oboe, Clarinet, Horn, Bassoon and Piano	1928	D
	Second Suite for Flute, Oboe, Clarinet, Horn,		
	and Bassoon	1922	D
Bridge, Frank	Divertimenti for Flute, Oboe, Clarinet and Bassoon	1938	D
	Dweller in My Deathless Dreams	1925	D
	Heart's Ease, piano solo	1921	D
	A Merry, Merry Xmas	1934	D
	The Pneu World, for Violoncello and Piano	n.d.	G
	Sonata for Piano and Violin	1933	CF
	String Quartet No. 3	1927	ESC
	String Quartet No. 4	1937	ESC
	Sextet for 2 Violins, 2 Violas, 2 Celli	1922	ESC
	Trio for Violin, Violoncello and Piano	1929	G
Britten, Benjamin	String Quartet in D Major, No. 1, Op. 25	1941	ESC
Burian, Hans	Five Lieder	1925	D
Burton, Stephen Douglas	Dances for Flute and Guitar	1983	CF
Busch, Adolph	Requiem for Mignon	1945	D
	Quartet in B Minor, Op. 59	1943	D
Caamaño, Roberto	Quinteto para piano y cuarteto de cuerdas	1962	CF
Carpenter, John Alden	Quintet for Piano and Strings	1933	ESC?
Casabona, Francisco	String Quartet in G Minor	1937	PFhm
Casella, Alfredo	Partita for Piano and Small Orchestra	1925	D
	Per Santa Elizabetta	1931	D

COMPOSER	TITLE	DATE	CATEGORY
	Sonata in C Major, Violoncello and Piano	1927	D
	Concerto Grosso in D Minor, Vivaldi transcription of "L'Estro armonico," No. 11	1936	D
	Los Poemas del Agua for nine instruments	1931	D
	Sonata à tre Arrangement of the Trio Sonata from The Musical Offering of J. S. Bach	1933	D
	Sonata à tre Transcription of Sammartini	n.d.	D
	Trio in D Major, arrangement of Muzio Clementi's Op. 27, No. 2	1932	D
	Sinfonia per pianoforte, clarinette, tromba e cello	19?	CF?
Castelnuovo-Tedesco, Mario	**Divertimento for Violin and Piano**	1945	G
	Per Santa Elizabetta	1931	D
	Quarteto in Sol	1929/30	ESC
Chávez, Carlos	**Ballet, Dark Meadow**	1944	CF
	Il [Segunda] invención, para violin, viola, y violoncello	1965	CF
Chevreuille, Raymond	**String Quartet No. 5**	1943	G
Clarke, Rebecca	**Rhapsody for 'Cello and Piano**	1923	ESC
	Sonata for Viola and Piano	1919	BPhm
	Trio for Violin, Violoncello, and Piano	1921	D
Collins, Anthony	**String Quartet No. 2**	1941	D
Copland, Aaron	**Appalachian Spring, Ballet for Martha**	1944	CF
	Appalachian Spring, Ballet reduction for Piano	1944	CF
	Quartet for Violin, Viola, Violoncello and Piano	1950	CF
Cordero, Roque	**String Quartet No. 1**	1960	CF
Corigliano, John	**Phantasmagoria** (on themes from "The Ghosts of Versailles" for 'cello and piano	1992	CF
Corti, Mario	**Tartini Concerto in A Major for String Orchestra and Cembalo.** Arranged for violin and piano	1924	D
Cowell, Henry	**String Quartet No. 5**	1956	CF
Creston, Paul	**Suite for Violoncello and Piano**	1956	CF
Crumb, George	**Ancient Voices of Children**	1970	C
Dallapiccola, Luigi	**Cinque canti per baritono e alcuni strumenti**	1957	CF
	Parole di San Paolo per una voce media e alcuni strumenti	1964	CF
	Sicut umbra, per una voce di cantate e quattro gruppi di strumenti	1970	CF

COMPOSER	TITLE	DATE	CATEGORY
Deak, Jon	**Vasilisa, A Young Girl Meets Baba-Yaga** For flute, oboe, violin, viola, violoncello, and piano	1994	CF
DeLamarter, Eric	**Terzetto for Violin, Viola, and Violoncello**	1911	D
Dello Joio, Norman	**The Lamentation of Saul,** for flute, oboe, clarinet, viola, cello, piano and baritone solo	1954	CF
Dick, Marcel	**String Quartet No. 2**	1938	D
Domange, Mme. Albert	**Suite for Violin and Piano**	1926	G
Eichheim, Henry	**Oriental Impressions: Chinese Sketch** For flute, oboe, violin, viola, harp and percussion	1921	G
	Oriental Impressions: Japanese Nocturne For small orchestra	1921	G
	Oriental Impressions: Japanese Sketch For flute, oboe, harp, and piano	1921	D
	Oriental Impressions: Nocturnal Impression of Peking For violin, viola, flute, oboe, harp, and piano	1921	G
	Sonata No. 2 for Violin and Piano	1934	D
Eloy, Jean-Claude	**Faisceaux-Diffractions**	1970	CF
Enesco, Georges	**Quartet in D Minor, Op. 30, No. 2, for** **Violin, Viola, Violoncello, and Piano**	1946	G
Farwell, Arthur	**String Quartet in A Major**	n.d.	G
Ficher, Jacobo	**String Quartet, Op. 35, No. 2**	1937	D
Fine, Irving	**Romanza for Wind Quintet**	1963	CF
Fine, Vivian	**Ode to Henry Purcell**	1984	CF
Finney, Ross Lee	**Quartet for Violin, Viola, Violoncello, and Piano**	1948	D
	String Quintet, For 2 violins, viola, 2 'celli	1959	CF
Fitelberg, Jerzy	**Quatrième quatour à cordes**	1936	CP
Franco, Johan	**Serenade Concertante**	1938	D
Frischenschlager, Friedrich	**Konzertante Musik, Op. 51** For piano and chamber orchestra	1931	D
Galindo, Blas	**Quinteto para instrumentos de arco y piano**	1960	CF
Gideon, Miriam	**Spirit Above the Dust**	1980	CF
Gilbert, Henry F.	**String Quartet**	n.d.	D
	Suite for Chamber Orchestra	1927	ESC
Ginastera, Alberto	**Bomarzo:** Cantata for narrator, baritone and orchestra	1964	CF
	Cuarteto de cuerdas, Op. 26	1968	CF
Goossens, Eugene	**Phantasy Sextet for Three Violins, Viola, and Two Violoncelli**	1923	ESC
	String Quartet, Op. 59, No. 2	1940	D
Grandjany, Marcel	**Aria: Piece in the Classic Style for Harp and Organ,** **Op. 19**	1940	D

COMPOSER	TITLE	DATE	CATEGORY
	Fantasie Chorale, Op. 21, on the hymn		
	Pange lingua corporis mysterium	1940	CF
	For harp and organ		
Green, Ray	**Concertante for Viola and Piano**	n.d.	D
Gruenberg, Louis	**Quartet, Op. 40, No. 2**	1937	CF
Guarnieri, Camargo	**String Quartet No. 3**	1962	CF
Gubaydulina, Sofiya	**Dancer on a Tightrope**	1993	CF
	For violin and piano		
Halffter, Cristobal	**Quartet II: Memories**	1970	CF
Hamilton, Iain	**Hyperion**	1977	CF
Hanson, Howard	**Four Psalms**	1964	CF
	Quartet, Op. 23, in One Movement	1923	ESC
Harris, Donald	**For the Night to Wear**	1978	CF
Harris, Roy	**Altissimi onnipotente (Canticle of the Sun)**	1961	CF
	Quintet for Two Violins, Two Violas and Violoncello	1940	CF
	Sonata for Violin and Piano (Sketches)	n.d.	G
	Three Variations on a Theme, Quartet No. 2	1933	CF
	Trio for Pianoforte, Violin and Violoncello	1934	CF
Harsányi, Tibor	**Aria, Cadenza, and Rondo**	1930	D
	For violoncello and orchestra		
Henry, Leigh	**Mistress Coolidge's Coronal, Chamber Pieces for Strings**	1930	D
Hill, Edward Burlingame	**Sextet for Flute, Oboe, Clarinet, Bassoon, Horn, and Piano, Op. 39**	1934	D
Hill, Mabel Wood	**Do Not Keep to Yourself, My Friend**	19?	D
	For voice and piano		
	Quintette for Oboe, Violin, Viola, Piano, and Voice	n.d.	G
Hindemith, Paul	**Canon à tre**	1949	D
	Hérodiade de Stéphane Mallarmé,	1944	CF
	Récitation Orchestrale, a Ballet		
	For chamber orchestra		
	Konzertmusik für Klavier, Blechbläser und Harfen	1930	ESC
	Four Part Songs to Old Texts	n.d.	G
Honegger, Arthur	**Concerto da Camera**	1948	D
	For flute, English horn, and string orchestra		
	Concerto da Camera, reduction for flute,		
	English horn, and piano	1948	D
	String Quartet No. 3	1936	D
Howe, Mary	**String Quartet**	n.d.	D
Hüttel, Josef	**Divertisment grotesque**	1929	CP
	For flute, oboe, clarinet, horn and piano		

COMPOSER	TITLE	DATE	CATEGORY
Huss, Henry Holden	**String Quartet in B Minor, Op. 31**	1918	D
Huybrechts, Albert	**Sonate pour violon et piano**	1926	CP
	Three Poems of Edgar Poe	1928	D
	Songs with piano		
Iarecki, Tadeusz	**Quartet for Strings, Op. 21**	1918	BP
Jacobi, Frederick	**Hagiographa: Three Biblical Narratives**		
	For String Quartet and Piano	1938	CF?
	Two Assyrian Prayers	1924	BPhm
	For soprano (or tenor) and chamber orchestra		
Kahn, Erich Itor	**Canon per Modum Speculi**	1945	D
	For soprano, alto, tenor and bass		
Kerntler, Jenö	**Sérénade for Violin, Violoncello, and Piano**	1932	G
Kirchner, Leon	**Trio for Violin, Cello and Piano**	1954	CF
Kolisch, Rudolf	**Happy Birthday to You**	1939	D
	For string quartet		
Kornsand, Emil	**String Quartet No. 2**	1944	D
Koutzen, Boris	**String Quartet No. 2**	1936	D
Kraft, William	**Music for String Quartet and Percussion**	1993	CF
Kroll, William	**Sextet for Two Violins, Two Violas, and Two Violoncellos**		
	Arrangement of Beethoven String Trio, Op. 9, No. 3	n.d.	D
Labroca, Mario	**String Quartet**	1923	D
Laderman, Ezra	**Double String Quartet**	1983	CF
Lajtha, Lázló	**String Quartet, Op. 11, No. 3**	n.d.	D
La Violette, Wesley	**Octet for Oboe, Clarinet, Bassoon, Horn, Viola,**		
	Violoncello, and Double Bass	1935	D
Llobet, Miguel	**Sept Chansons Populaires Espagñoles**		
	by Manuel de Falla, arranged for guitar accompaniment	1931	ESC
Lockwood, Normand	**Trio for Flute, Viola, and Harp**	1939	D
Loeffler, Charles Martin	**Canticum fratris solis**	1925	CF
	For voice and chamber orchestra		
	Partita for Piano and Violin	1930	CF
Lopatnikov, Nikolai	**String Quartet No. 2**	n.d.	D
Malipiero, Gian Francesco	**Cantàri alla Madrigalesca**	1931	D
	Concerto for Orchestra	1931	D
	Epodi e Giambi	1932	D
	Cinque favole per una voce e piccola orchestra	1950	CF
	La Nave della Vittoria, Ricercare No. 2	1926	D
	For flute, oboe, clarinet, bassoon, horn, three violas, and double bass		
	Per Santa Elizabetta	1931	D

COMPOSER	TITLE	DATE	CATEGORY
	Quattro Vecchie Canzoni For solo voice with flute, oboe, clarinet, bassoon, horn, viola and double bass	1940	D
	Rispetti e strambotti For string quartet	1920	BP
	Sonata à cinque For flute, violin, viola, violoncello, and piano	1934	D
	Sonata à tre for Violin, Violoncello and Piano	1927	D
	Quarteto di Elizabetta	1963	CF
	Sonata à quattro per flauto, oboe, clarineto, e fagotto	1954	CF
	Stornelli e Ballate For string quartet	1923	D
	String Quartet No. 4	1934	D
	I Trionfi d'Amore; tre commedie in una Opera, vocal score with piano	1931	D
Malipiero, Riccardo	**In Time of Daffodils**	1964	CF
Martino, Donald	**String Quartet**	1983	CF
Martinů, Bohuslav	**Quintet for Two Violins, Two Violas, and Violoncello**	1927	D
	Sextet for Two Violins, Two Violas, and Two Violoncelli	1932	CP
Massarani, Renzo	**Pastorale for Oboe, Viola, Bassoon, and Violoncello**	1923	D
Matsudaira, Yoritsune	**Rhapsodie on a Theme of Gagaku**	1982	CF
Mennin, Peter	**Sonata Concertante for Violin and Piano**	1956	CF
Menotti, Gian Carlo	**The Unicorn, the Gorgon, and the Manticore**	1956	CF
Messiaen, Olivier	**Woodwind Sextet**	1958	CF
Migot, Georges	**Le Premier Livre de Divertissements** **Français à deux et à trois**	1925	D
Milhaud, Darius	**Jacob's Dream, Suite chorégraphique en cinq parties** For oboe, violin, viola, violoncello and double bass	1949	CF
	Jeux de Printemps, Ballet suite For chamber orchestra	1944	CF
	String Quartet No. 8	1932	D
	String Quartet No. 9	1935	D
	String Quartet No. 10	1940	D
	Septour à cordes	1940	CF?
Mitchel, Lyndol C.	**String Quartet in E Minor**	1958	CF
Mojsisovics, Roderich von	**Es wird Früling!, Op. 18, No. 3** Song with piano	1931	G
Nabokov, Nicolas	**Serenata estiva** For string quartet	1937	D
Nono, Luigi	**Sará dolce tacere**	1960	CF
Ornstein, Leo	**Quintet for Two Violins, Viola, Violoncello and Piano, Op. 92**	1929	D

COMPOSER	TITLE	DATE	CATEGORY
Orrego-Salas, Juan	**Palabras de Don Quixote**	1970	CF
Page, George Nelson	**Sonata in F Minor, Op. 7, for Piano**	1926	D
Palmer, Robert	**Quartet for Violin, Viola, Violoncello and Piano**	1946	D
	Quintet for Two Violins, Viola, Violoncello, and Piano	1950	CF
Perle, George	**Windows of Order, String Quartet No. 8**	1988	CF
Petit, Raymond	**Trois Récits des Evangiles**		
	For tenor voice and string quartet	n.d.	G
Petrassi, Goffredo	**String Trio**	1960	CF
Phillips, Burrill	**String Quartet No. 2**	1958	CF
Pierné, Gabriel	**Sonate da Camera, Op. 48**		
	For flute, violoncello, and piano	1926	G
Piston, Walter	**Partita for Violin, Viola, and Organ**	1944	CF
	Quintet for Wind Instruments	1956	CF
	Sextet for Strings	1964	CF
	Trio for Violin, Violoncello, and Piano	1935	CF
Pizzetti, Ildebrando	**Epithalamium**	1939	CF
	Cantata for solo voices, chorus and small orchestra		
	String Quartet in D	1933	D
	Tre Canzoni	1928	D
	For voice and string quartet		
	Trio in A for Violin, Violoncello, and Piano	1925	CF
Porter, Quincy	**String Quartet No. 7**	1943	D
Poulenc, Francis	**Sonata for Flute and Piano**	1957	CF
Powell, Mel	**Cantilena**	1970	CF
Prokofiev, Sergei	**String Quartet Op. 50**	1930	CF
Raksin, David	**Oedipus Memneitai**	1986	CF
	For baritone solo, chorus and chamber orchestra		
Ravel, Maurice	**Chansons Madécasses,**		
	For voice, flute, cello, and piano	1925	CF
Reiser, Alois	**Quartet in E minor, Op. 16**	1918	BP
	String Quartet in C, Op. 18	1930	D
Respighi, Ottorino	**Concerto à cinque**	1933	D
	For oboe, trumpet, violin, double bass, piano, and string orchestra		
	The Fountains of Rome (Sketches)	n.d.	G
	Per Santa Elizabetta	1931	D
	Trittico Botticelliano	1927	D
	For chamber orchestra		
Riegger, Wallingford	**La Belle Dame sans Merçi**	1924	BP
	For strings, oboe (English horn), clarinet, horn, and four solo voices (soprano, mezzo, tenor, and bass)		

COMPOSER	TITLE	DATE	CATEGORY
	Three Canons for Woodwinds	1930	D
	For piccolo, flute, clarinet, oboe and bassoon		
	Two Canons for Woodwinds	1930	D
	For piccolo, flute, oboe, clarinet, and bassoon		
Rochberg, George	**Trio for Violin, Cello, and Piano**	1985	CF
Röntgen, Julius	**String Quartet. Heer Halewÿn Zong een Liedekÿn**	1922	BPhm
Rogati, George	**Sonata for Violin and Piano**	1924	D
Rogister, Jean	**Quintet for Clavecin, Two Quintons,**		
	Viola d'Amor and Viola da Gamba	1934	D
	String Quartet in D, No. 4	1927	D
Rootham, Cyril Bradley	**Septet for Viola, Oboe, Clarinet, Bassoon, Horn, Flute, and Harp**	n.d.	D
Rorem, Ned	**Nantucket Songs**	1979	CF
Rosé, Alfred	**String Quartet**	1927	D
Roth, Feri	**String Quartet in D**	1932	D
Roussel, Albert	**Trio for Flute, Viola, and Violoncello, Op. 40**	1929	D
Rubinstein, Beryl	**String Quartet in D♭ No. 2**	1933	D
Saygun, Adnan	**String Quartet, Op. 35**	1958	CF
Schoenberg, Arnold	**String Quartet No. 3**	1927	CF
	String Quartet No. 4	1936	CF
Schuller, Gunther	**Music for Brass Quintet**	1961	CF
Schuman, William	**Amaryllis**	1964	CF
	For string trio		
	Night Journey (Work for Martha Graham)	1948	CF
	For orchestra		
	String Quartet No. 4	1950	CF
Sessions, Roger	**String Quartet in E Minor, No. 1**	1936	D
Shapey, Ralph	**Trilogy: Song of Songs No. 1**	1980	CF
Siegmeister, Elie	**Ways of Love**	1983	CF
Simon, James	**Legende für Streichquartett in Drei Sätzen**	1930	D
Smith, David Stanley	**Sonata in A for Violin and Piano, Op. 51**	1924	D
	String Quartet in C, Op. 46	1920	D
	String Quartet in E♭, Op. 57	1927	D
	String Quartet in C, Op. 71, No. 6	1934	D
	String Quartet in A, Op. 77, No. 8	1936	D
	String Quartet, Op. 90, No. 10	n.d.	D
Sowerby, Leo	**Serenade for String Quartet**	1917	D
	Trio for Flute, Viola, and Piano	1919	G

COMPOSER	TITLE	DATE	CATEGORY
Stock, Frederick	**Rhapsodic Fantasy for Orchestra**	1925	CF
	Two Movements from String Quartet		
	(by Elizabeth Sprague Coolidge, arranged for string orchestra)	1916	D
Stravinsky, Igor	**Apollon Musagète**	1928	CF
	Ballet in two scenes		
Strube, Gustav	**Quintet for Flute, Oboe, Clarinet, Horn, and Bassoon**	1930	D
	Sonata for Violoncello and Piano	n.d.	D
Szántó, Théodore	**Nuits Blanches**	1931	D
	For small orchestra		
	Suite Choréographique	1929	G
	For string quartet		
Tal, Josef	**Imago**	1982	CF
	For chamber orchestra		
Tansman, Alexandre	**Serenade No. 3 for Orchestra**	1943	ESC
	Sonata No. 4 for Piano	1941	D
	Triptyque for String Quartet	1930	D
Tertis, Lionel	**Variations on the Passsacaglia of Handel**		
	(From Suite No. 7), for two Violas	1935	D
Thompson, Randall	**String Quartet No. 1**	1941	D
Thomson, Virgil	**Pervigilium Veneris (The Feast of Love)**	1964	CF
Toch, Ernst	**Quintet for Two Violins, Viola, Violoncello, and Piano, Op. 64**	1938	ESC
	Trio for Violin, Viola, and Violoncello, Op. 63	1938	D
Tuthill, Burnet Corwin	**Fantasy Sonata in One Movement for Clarinet and Piano, Op. 3**	1932	D
Uray, Ludwig	**Suite in A Major for Violin and Piano**	n.d.	D
Vega, Aurelio de la	**Structures for String Quartet**	1962	CF
Villa-Lobos, Heitor	**Trio for Violin, Viola, and Violoncello**	1945	CF
Warner, H. Waldo	**Suite for Violin, Violoncello, and Piano, Op. 22**	1921	BP
Webern, Anton	**Quartet, Op. 28**	1938	CF
Weiner, Leo	**String Quartet No. 2 in F# minor**	1922	BP
Wellesz, Egon	**String Quartet, Op. 60**	1943	G
Wernick, Richard	**String Quartet No. 3**	1989	CF
White, Eric Walter	**Three Songs for Medium Voice**	1925	D
White, Willy	**String Quartet in A Minor**	1938	D
Wigglesworth, F.	**Song for a Child**	1943	G
	With piano accompaniment		
Wildschut, Clara	**Sonata for Violin and Piano**	1926	D
Woollen, Russell	**Lines of Stephen Crane**	1981	CF

About the Author

Cyrilla Barr has for many years written and lectured on the popular religious music of medieval Italy. Her work on the subject is well known to musicologists and historians of the period. Despite the pleasure of spending summers in Italy doing research, practicality eventually dictated finding a topic closer to home that could be researched during the time that teaching required her presence in Washington. She looked to the obvious place, the Library of Congress, for a topic to develop into a short journal article and chose as her subject Elizabeth Sprague Coolidge. The rest, as the saying goes, is history.

Emerson once ventured the opinion that "Properly speaking there is no such thing as history—only biography." Tracking the continuity of one human life in a way illuminates the larger patterns of history, forming traceries that highlight details too easily lost on the larger tapestries of time. In Coolidge's case the exercise is unusually rewarding for her life spanned not only extraordinary advances in science and technology, but also a great diversity of styles and "isms" in music. This monograph explores that life briefly, concentrating on her pioneering role in involving the U.S. government in patronage of the arts through the agency of the Library of Congress.

In the ten years that have passed since Professor Barr began working on Coolidge that "short paper" has grown into a full-length biography soon to be published by Schirmer Books; a book on the subject of women patrons, edited with Ralph Locke; various journal articles on Coolidge; and this monograph—all proof of what a compelling subject Elizabeth Sprague Coolidge is.

Cyrilla Barr is currently chairperson of the musicology department of the Benjamin T. Rome School of Music of the Catholic University of America. She has done graduate study at the University of Wisconsin, the Eastman School of Music, Università per Stranieri, Perugia, Italy, the University of Florence, and earned her doctorate from the Catholic University of America. Honors include a Fulbright Scholarship and an I Tatti Fellowship to Harvard University's Center for Italian Renaissance Studies in Florence, as well as awards from the American Council of Learned Societies and the National Endowment for the Humanities. She has lectured widely in this country and Europe and has twice received Catholic University's Outstanding Teacher Award.